IMAGES
of America

CRYSTAL PALACE
MARKET

IMAGES
of America

CRYSTAL PALACE
MARKET

Manushi Mathur

ARCADIA
PUBLISHING

Published by Arcadia Publishing
Charleston, South Carolina

Printed in the United States of America

Library of Congress Control Number: 2023935832

For all general information, please contact Arcadia Publishing:
Telephone 843-853-2070
Fax 843-853-0044
E-mail sales@arcadiapublishing.com

Visit us on the Internet at www.arcadiapublishing.com

This book is dedicated to my mother, Anamika Mathur.

CONTENTS

ACKNOWLEDGMENTS

I am grateful to my husband for being my biggest supporter and encouraging me throughout the journey of writing this book. I owe my heartfelt thanks to the helpful librarians and historians at the San Francisco History Center and the San Francisco Public Library. There were a tremendous amount of research hurdles that came during the writing and researching of this book during the COVID pandemic, and I am truly thankful for these online historical collections that helped me in my initial research: the Library of Congress Digital Collections and the California Digital Newspaper collections. Unless otherwise noted, all images appear courtesy of the San Francisco History Center, Digital Collections, and the California Digital Newspaper collections.

INTRODUCTION

The Crystal Palace Market was a large city market built in 1922 on Eighth and Market Streets in San Francisco conceptualized and built by the Rousseau brothers: Arthur and Oliver Rousseau. It was a massive steel-framed structure lit by skylights designed by the architect David C. Coleman. It functioned as a one-stop marketplace for the everyday needs of the people of San Francisco for 37 years. It contained dairy stands, meat markets, fruits and vegetable stands, caterers and shops selling exotic produce, appliances, beauty parlors, pet salons, and record stores. It was a place where several local family businesses thrived and had the opportunity to build a strong retail community. This business community in the later years, advocated for labor laws which brought significant changes in the business practices in the city. The Crystal Palace Market was also one of the first large-scale supermarkets in San Francisco that was extensively marketed to the San Francisco community.

The land on which the market was constructed had a rich history of being a public space used by the citizens since 1874. The first building on this land was used as a Mechanic's Pavilion and hosted annual mechanics' and manufacturers' fairs. In 1881, this building was demolished to make way for the Central Park baseball venue, which hosted several prominent baseball teams from 1881 to 1898. The baseball venue was succeeded by the construction of the Central Theatre in the 1900s, a popular venue hosting melodramas and theater. During the devastating earthquake of 1906, this building burned down. Post-earthquake, the corner of Eighth and Market Streets was initially used for tent theaters, which brought back the memories of Central Theater for the public and showcased the resilience of the people of San Francisco. This corner of Eighth and Market Streets was frequently in the news from 1908 to 1922 for hosting circus troupes and carnivals with massive parades on the Market Street inviting spectators from all over the city and the bay area. The attention that the carnivals and circus troupes got in the local San Francisco newspapers made the location of Eighth and Market Streets more popular among the public. The street was accessible by streetcars, thus making the location a prime spot for prominent public buildings like San Francisco City Hall. In 1922, the developer and contractor Oliver M. Rousseau and his brother, Arthur, purchased the land aiming to build a massive city market that would replace the corner grocery store.

The Crystal Palace Market was frequently advertised before the opening and housed more than 300 store owners who leased the marketplace in 1922. The construction of significant entertainment centers like the Orpheum Theatre, which opened in 1926 on the location on Eighth and Market Streets, brought more foot traffic to the market, thus making this location frequented by thousands of people on a daily basis. The Crystal Palace Market was also the first large-scale market with hundreds of assigned parking spaces for its patrons and frequent shopping shuttles dropping customers off at its 22 entrances making it significant to the transportation history of the city.

Author Gus Lee, in his book *China Boy*, reminisces about his childhood days visiting Market Street and the Crystal Palace Market, talking about the immense scale of the market and the variety of goods that the Crystal Palace Market offered, making it a place where a person could find anything ranging from various types of foods to appliances to home decor. He says, "He took me to the Crystal Palace Market. It faced the city hall fountains and the underground construction of Brooks Hall. It was another cathedral, more of glass than concrete, airy, spacious, its glass-latticed, domed ceiling beyond the reach of my eyes. The Palace was an emporium dedicated to the palates of the cosmos. It probably had food from Saturn. It was the FAO Schwarz of the stomach. It was so big and so full of edibles that I recognized it as the true cathedral to human existence. Rows and rows of food of every type and variety, from Jakarta, Juan de Fuca, Antwerp, Leeds, Vienna, and Singapore. Canned goods, fresh produce, fishmongers, breads, pastas, legumes of every variety. I was in Heaven, smelling everything, grinning from east to west with the salivary promise of an upended cornucopia. I was ready to eat it all, the wrappings, the glass containers, the windows in the walls." As the years went by, the Crystal Palace Market hosted seasonal sales, events like Christmas celebrations, and live music, which were attended by thousands of people. On August 1, 1959, after 37 years of being in service, the Crystal Palace Market closed its doors. It was demolished to make room for the new $8 million, 400-room Del Webb's Townehouse. In 2021, the largest Whole Foods Market in San Francisco was constructed on the same site where the Crystal Palace Market once existed and served the people of San Francisco.

One

THE PREDECESSORS

The four-acre lot at Eighth and Market Street had been a witness of several significant events in San Francisco's history since the 1870s. In 1874, the fifth Mechanics Institute Pavilion was built on this land. This big shed-like structure ran 550 feet long and 200 feet deep and fronted Market Street and extended along the east side of Eighth Street to Mission Street. There were several mechanics' and manufacturers' fairs held here. This photograph from 1883 is of Second Street Ignatius Church & College at the extreme left in the distance, old San Francisco City Hall before the construction of the dome near Seventh Street, and Mechanics Pavilion on Eighth and Market Streets.

The Mechanics Institute Pavilion functioned until 1881, when the institute decided to move its pavilion to a larger site in another part of the city. The pavilion was demolished in 1811, and Central Park was built, becoming the cradle of baseball history in San Francisco. This is a photograph of Central Park in 1896. The Central Park opened in 1884 and held approximately 15,000 fans of baseball and other sports. In 1888, it became the home of the newly formed California State League. Over the years, this location became known for exhibitions/panoramas and theaters.

In the early 1900s, the Central Park was closed and this location became the home of the Central Theatre, which became a celebrated venue for theater, art, and drama until the 1906 earthquake, when it was destroyed completely. Pictured here is a newspaper article from the *San Francisco Call* on December 13, 1900, showing an artistic sketch of the proposed brick and stone front of the Central Theater. The article describes the issue regarding its opening due to the refusal of permits from the Department of Public Works, stating that the theater had all the necessary safety standards for public safety.

Pictured here is the news article from the *San Francisco Call* published on December 23, 1900, announcing the opening of the Central Theatre. The new Central Theatre opened with the production of David Belasco's war drama *The Heart of Maryland*. The article describes that the seating capacity of the theater was 2,000 and that it had one of the largest stages in the city, at 53 by 95 feet. The ground floor of the Central Theater was occupied with orchestral seats, and the second floor was devoted to a parquet circle and twelve draped proscenium boxes. The article describes the interior of the theater as cream-colored and the ceilings frescoed with bold Cupid designs. The Central Theatre, after its opening in 1900, became one of the most popular theater and drama venues in the city. During this period, Market Street became one of the significant roads, which was lined with theaters and entertainment venues.

In 1906, the devastating Great Earthquake and Fire hit San Francisco and nearly destroyed 80 percent of the city including the Central Theater on Eighth and Market Streets. The Great Earthquake took place at 5:12 a.m. on the morning of April 18, 1906. This earthquake also destroyed the old San Francisco City Hall, a structure costing $7 million, which was first wrecked by the earthquake and then destroyed by fire. Pictured here are the ruins of the Central Theatre, which was badly burned down in the 1906 fire along with several buildings along Market Street.

The Great Earthquake and Fire ruined almost every building along Market Street with the second tremor and multiple tremors in the later days making already fragile buildings fall down completely. Amid the rubble of stones, bricks, and metal, thousands of San Francisco citizens died, and hundreds were injured. Several buildings in other parts of the city, like the opera house, were also destroyed by the fire. Pictured here are the destroyed cobblestone road of Market Street and completely burned blocks.

This is a photograph of the Central Theatre, seen on the right, burned down along with a number of significant public buildings like the St. Ignatius Church & College on Market Street in the 1906 Great Earthquake and Fire. The burnt and fallen bricks and damaged roads can be seen in this image, showing the massive impact of this earthquake on public and private properties. The earthquake and fire destroyed all of San Francisco's prominent theaters and playhouses, including the Majestic, Columbia, Orpheum, and Grand Opera House, which were a mass of ruins. The earthquake left hundreds of citizens homeless with scarcity of water and food. It was estimated that about 50,000 refugees fled to nearby cities because of this earthquake, as reported by the *Los Angeles Times* on April 19, 1906.

The Great Earthquake completely wrecked the Chronicle building, the Examiner building, and the Hobart building and severely damaged the Palace Hotel building, one of the most prominent buildings on the Market Street frequented by the public. The city witnessed a complete demolition of the Business District on Market Street. The burned district extended from the waterfront south of Market Street to Market Street and west to Eleventh Street, north of Market. The fire extended out Hayes and McAllister Streets nearly to Fillmore, from the waterfront along Market to Montgomery Street, and north from the waterfront to Montgomery. Several manufactories, hotels, wholesale houses, and residences comprising the principal part of the business quarters were destroyed in the fire. Pictured here are the ruins and damages witnessed by multiple iconic buildings on Market Street in 1906 with rescue operations in full swing.

As the days progressed, post the earthquake, massive fires throughout the city eventually broke out and completely demolished several buildings along Market Street. Pictured here is a building in complete ruins and people fleeing in the background in 1906. The *San Francisco Call* on April 21, 1906, reported that "the city will rise again in splendor." It also said, "San Francisco has demonstrated the courage and confidence of her citizens by declaring to the world that assistance will not be solicited from cities other than those in California. The spirit of the hour is that the city will rise again in renewed splendor and in such form that the dream of beautiful San Francisco will be realized."

View out Market Street from the Ferry Tower, taken shortly after the fire, showing the railroad tracks being laid temporarily on Market Street to facilitate the removal of debris

Pictured here is the view from the ferry building shortly after the fire in 1906 with the city in shambles after the massive earthquake and fire. Soon after the fire, the city sprang into action to restore roads and other infrastructure. Railroad tracks were laid temporarily to restart transportation within the city and facilitate the removal of debris.

Pictured here is a photograph from 1908 showing Market Street slowly being rebuilt and revived through public events like parades.

Post-earthquake, the city was inclined to bounce back from the tragedy. There were news articles in newspapers from 1906 discussing the coming of canvas theaters in San Francisco to bring back theater and art for the citizens. There were two such tent theaters introduced in the city post the earthquake, with one on the site of the Central Theater on Market and Eighth Streets and one smaller tent at the site of the Majestic Theater on Ninth and Market Streets.

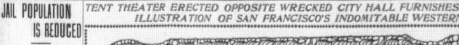

JAIL POPULATION IS REDUCED

NUMBER NOW LESS THAN FOR PAST FOUR YEARS

Only 92 Names Are on the Books, Whereas One Night Last Winter Jailer McCaulley Entertained 200 Visitors

TENT THEATER ERECTED OPPOSITE WRECKED CITY HALL FURNISHES ILLUSTRATION OF SAN FRANCISCO'S INDOMITABLE WESTERN SPIRIT

DEVISE SCHEME TO GET SCH

SCIENCE HIGH BIDS S WITHIN LIMIT

Arroyo Seco Building to Be E Affording Better Educatio Facilities in That Vicinity

SISTERS' INSTITUTE

PROGRAM ARRANGED

SUES FOR BREACH OF PR

Pictured here is an article from *the Los Angeles Sunday Herald* discussing the creation of tent theaters on the corner of Eighth and Market Streets to revive the corner where the Central Theater stood. The article talks about the unwavering spirit of San Francisco and how the old Central Theater's blood-curling melodramatic reproductions were replaced by first-class productions in this new tent theater. The tent theater measured 90 by 200 feet and was 38 feet high, with the stage of the tent theater measuring 45 by 120 feet.

RAYS PLANNING SMOKER AND TRIP EAST

CIRCUS IN TOWN WITH TANGO HORSE! HURRY, KIDS, HURRY

BORG PAINTING WILL BE SOLD AT AUCTION

Madame Bedini and her tango horse, who appears in Robinson's Circus.

RAYS PLANNING SMOKER AND TRIP EAST

celebration of the twenty-sixth anniversary of their organization, the California Grays will give a smoker for their members and their friends, Tuesday evening, May 9. This affair will also be in the nature of a house warming for the new headquarters of the organization in the Exposition Auditorium, where the smoker will be held.

The California Grays are making preparations for their trip to Washington, where they have been invited to participate in the presidential inaugural March.

"In accepting this invitation," said Captain Cyrus F. Voorhies, commander of the Grays, "we decided to make the trip to exploit the resources, industries and attractions of San Francisco and California.

CONGRATULATIONS FROM MAYOR

When he heard of the invitation to the Grays, Mayor James Rolph Jr. wrote Captain Voorhies, saying: "You will do the state and city credit in the great East, and San Francisco will be proud of you, as she is always."

Milton T. Clark, chairman of the committee in charge of the arrangements for the trip, said today:

"We expect to take about 100 men and a band of 30 pieces with several cars containing exhibits of California products.

Stops will be made at all the principal cities along the route both going and returning. We shall have a lecturer with stereopticon views, who will speak at all stopping places in connection with military drills and band concerts, which will be free to the public. In this way we intend to follow up the publicity that was gained through the Exposition."

HONOR FOR CALIFORNIA

At their last assemblage, Captain Sam Servance, U. S. A., retired, addressed the Grays on "Military Training for Americans," and he will assist the Grays instructions while they are preparing for the Eastern trip.

"It is the first time any California organization has been invited to take part in an inaugural parade in Washington, and the project has been endorsed with enthusiasm by prominent men and organized bodies in the city. Secretary of the Interior Franklin K. Lane wrote: "I think it a splendid idea." Congressman Julius Kahn interested himself in obtaining the invitation, and Congressman John I. Nolan wrote: "I do not hesitate in saying that the people of San Francisco as well as the people of the state of California would greatly benefit from the tour."

MANY JOIN IN PRAISE

Civic Center and Hub of Universe Moved to Eighth and Market; Parade Tomorrow

It's one May Day right after another for San Francisco's youngsters. The John Robinson circus is here, for the first time in thirty years, and as far as little San Francisco goes—and a good share of big San Francisco, for that matter—the Civic Center, and the hub

THIS BOY LANDS!

Letter On Circus Misses Contest, But Treat's On The Call

WANTS ICE CREAM

BORG PAINTING WILL BE SOLD AT AUCTION

An exhibition of more than 100 paintings by Carl Oscar Borg, which is now in progress on the ground floor of the Nutall Building, 314 Sutter street, will close tomorrow afternoon at 2 o'clock with an auction sale. Borg, who has made his home in California for more than fifteen years, is about to start on a two years' study trip to Arizona, where he will paint pictures of the desert and of Indian life.

The present exhibition represents every type of painting. There are landscapes called from Europe, Africa, Asia and America; there are marine scenes and portraits. Borg is a painter of unusual versatility and has won high honors in Paris, London, Rome and Petersburg. He was awarded a silver medal recently at the Exposition, where a number of his works were shown in the Swedish collection.

Borg has made a reputation for himself for his original conception of things. His stroke is bold, and, at times, may even look impudent to the occasional observer. He is strictly an impressionist and paints things as he sees them. His street scene from Assuan, landscapes from Honduras and steppes from Asia Minor are considered among his best works of their kind.

The exhibits which are to be auctioned off tomorrow represent the work of seven years and include the paintings which were shown in France, Italy and Russia.

Posses Hunt Slayer Of Girl and Fathe

By Associated Press.
THOMPSON, Conn., May 2—George A. Pettis, a well-to-do farmer, and his daughter, Sybil, were shot to death at their home here today. Deputy sheriffs and a posse are searching for John Elliott, who is charged with the shooting.

Refusal of the daughter to receive Elliott's attention is believed to have been the motive for the shooting.

Elliott is alleged to have fired the shots through a window, after having cut the telephone wires to prevent a call for help being sent out from the house.

$200,000 FIRE IN RALEIGH

RALEIGH, N. C., May 2—Fire in the business section here early today destroyed seven buildings, with an estimated loss of $200,000.

BLACKHEADS GO QUICK BY THIS SIMPLE METHO

After the tent theaters, the corner of Eighth and Market Streets served as a ground for circus troupes and carnivals until 1922. The newspaper *San Francisco Call and Post* on May 2, 1916, describes the spectacle on Eighth and Market Streets. The city celebrated the return of the John Robinson Circus and made way for the dazzling performers of the parade, including the famous Madame Bedini and her tango horse.

The site of Eighth and Market Streets also became a site where several prominent parades happened, and by 1922, it had become a hub of several prominent public and private buildings. Pictured here is a parade on Market Street. The Rialto Theater and Jewel Theater can be seen in the background.

Two

THE GRAND OPENING

In 1922, the developer and contractor Oliver M. Rousseau and his brother Arthur purchased the land on Eighth and Market Streets and conceptualized it as the biggest food market in San Francisco. Pictured on the left is a newspaper clipping from June 6, 1922, in the *Colusa Daily Sun*, a local newspaper from Colusa County, 65 miles north of Sacramento. The article talks about the new one-million-square-foot Crystal Palace Market, which the newspaper claims is the largest public market in the world.

S. F. TO BUILD LARGEST PUBLIC MARKET

SAN FRANCISCO, June 6—The announcement was made here today by the organizers of the $1,000,000 Crystal Palace market to be erected in this city, the largest public market in the world, that A. D. Stewart had been retained as general manager to take immediate charge of all preliminary work toward securing tenants, defining the policy of the market and its conduct when completed. The retention of Stewart, who is nationally known in the groceries and wholesale lines and is an authority whose contributions on trade matters frequently appear in the leading publications, was in line with the policy adopted by the Oakland market in securing the services of a prominent figure in Martin Madsen, former secretary to Governor Stephens, and the 12th and Market street market in that city in securing the services of H. S. Maddox, former head of the division of markets of the state department of agriculture.

The Crystal Palace market will cover 95,000 feet of floor space, almost a city block in area, and will be located at Eighth and Market streets, the hub of the city's transportation lines. The work of securing tenants is now under way and construction is expected to begin in about two months.

The Rousseau brothers conceived the Crystal Palace Market as a one-of-a-kind market in this iconic location, with 95,000 feet of floor space selling everything from high-quality produce to sporting goods to appliances in the later years. It was aimed to replace the corner grocery store.

Pictured here is the new Crystal Palace Market under construction in 1922. This photograph was taken by newspapers to show the new developments on Market Street and how rapidly the land along Market Street was developing.

UPPER MARKET NEW SHOP CENTER

Attention of the San Francisco investors, real estate dealers, together with the retail merchants, is being directed to upper Market street, especially between Seventh and Eighth. Many new buildings and improvements to sites in that locality are rapidly transferring upper Market street into an added shopping center.

A. F. Rousseau has recently invested more than $2,000,000 in buildings for store purposes and lofts for retail trade. The Crystal Palace Market will be a part of the unit of six store buildings in this vicinity.

W. G. Wagnon is investing more than $200,000 in a new store building in this locality.

Nearly all of the 175 departments of the Crystal Palace Market al-

FACTORY PLANT OPENING HELD

The factory property was purchased during the war period and is situated in the heart of the warehousing and manufacturing district. This section is rapidly filling up with modern factories and warehouses.

The company, which is established in New York, Rahway, N. J.; Chicago, Montreal, London and San Francisco, manufactures Magnolia anti-friction metal, all grades of white metal alloys, type metals and special formulae metal.

ready have been leased. Owners of the property are investigating the records of all applicants for departments with the hope of maintaining a high standard type of merchants in the new upper Market shopping district.

This newspaper clipping from October 21, 1922, in the *San Francisco Call and Post* is reflective of one of the forms of advertisements in prominent local newspapers calling retail merchants and real estate investors in developing the area of upper Market Street between Seventh and Eighth Streets. The opening of the Crystal Palace Market was instrumental in bringing more real estate investment to this area of the city. The *San Francisco Call and Post* on September 16, 1922, also reported that the 175 leases for different stores were sold out within a matter of months, even before the steel and concrete foundations were laid.

The Crystal Palace Market was marketed in leading newspapers like the *San Francisco Call and Post* as the largest market in the city with over 175 departments and stores with the length of counters a mile in extent. Pictured here is the facade of the new Crystal Palace Market in the *San Francisco Call and Post* on September 2, 1922.

The Crystal Palace Market was named after the historic Crystal Palace in London. The architect for this massive steel-framed building lit by skylights was David C. Coleman. Pictured here is the iconic facade of the Crystal Palace Market. The cornerstone for the Crystal Palace Market was laid on Eighth and Market Streets on October 5, 1922. The event was attended by government dignitaries and included a musical program.

Pictured here is the advertisement announcing the formal opening of the Crystal Palace Market on December 14, 1922, in the *San Francisco Call and Post*. The Crystal Palace Market was advertised as a Christmas gift to the people of San Francisco. It was heavily advertised as an affordable market for people of all budgets.

NICIPAL BUS INE BIDS TO BE OPENED MONDAY

Board of Supervisors at its
meeting will receive bids for a
e to be operated in the Em-
ro from Third and Townsend
to the foot of Van Ness

will be received Monday on
basis for the privilege and
ll also be received on supply-
city with buses.

meeting yesterday of the
and public utilities commit-
was decided to go ahead with
mbarcadero line, which has
ndorsed by a number of civic
zations and the waterfront
ies.

TUDY LEGAL PHASES

to the receiving of the bids
ngineer M. M. O'Shaughnessy
y Attorney George Lull today
lding a series of conferences
de the legal phases of the line
cide what rules shall govern
ration. Among the decisions
ade are whether the bus shall
ned by one or two men,
r a 5 or 10 cent fare shall be
d and other questions.
nsions of lines on the Munic-
stem were sidetracked tem-
y to give preference to a meet-
ay in the City Hall to discuss
posal of the purchase of the
Street Railroad system.
y's meeting was a special
torial one, open to discussion
ams.

LINES AFFECTED

proposed extension lines af-
by the postponement in favor
ay's meeting are the Sunset
ion View.
rman John McGregor urged
pening of construction work
hich street immediately as a
f the Sunset extension at pre-
. This work will
the tunnel work under
Vista Park.
Ocean View extension was
in order to allow citizens in
strict to hold a series of meet-
get a universal expression
desires. These meetings will
d and at a future date they
port their wishes regarding
9,000 extension project to the
sors.

*Ganna Walska, famous Po-
lish opera star and bride of
Harold McCormick, who
has purchased a theater in
the French capital.—International Newsreel photo.*

WALSKA BUYS PARIS THEATER

PARIS, Dec. 14 (By International
News Service, by Radio).— Ganna
Walska, famous Polish grand opera
singer and wife of Harold McCormick, Chicago multi-millionaire, has
purchased the Champs Elysee Theater, it was announced today.

Total of more than $200,000,000
fire insurance paid out in the United
States in 1921 went to firebugs.

CEREMONY AND MUSIC OPEN NEW MARKET

San Francisco's new market, the
Crystal Palace, was formally thrown
open to the public today, complete in
every detail.

The great building of concrete and
glass that has been in the course of
construction at Eighth and Market
streets for the last six months was
dedicated by city officials and offi-
cers of the A. F. Rousseau Syndi-
cate, the organization that launched
the venture.

Dr. William C. Hassler, city health
officer, threw open the doors of the
Market street entrance this morning.

To the accompaniment of bands,
Dr. Hassler entered the building.
With him were members of the market company and John C. Horgan,
chief building inspector of the city.

IN 'RUNNING ORDER'

After the official party, great
crowds of San Franciscans swarmed
into the building to find everything
in perfect order as if the market had
been in operation for months.

Proprietors of stalls were behind
their counters ready to sell the
things they are to specialize in. The
giant refrigerating plant of the market, one of the largest in the coun-
try, was functioning for the benefit
of the heaps of vegetables and fruits.

This afternoon another ceremony
in the opening exercises took place.
Mayor Rolph presided at a recep-
tion and made a speech welcom-
ing the market, which it is expected
will benefit San Francisco greatly in
an economical way.

PARKING ARRANGED

Throughout the day a band played.
All functions of the market
were carried on. The numerous
call boys—a unique feature of the
Crystal Palace—were on hand to
carry the bundles of purchasers to
their machines and to the street
cars. Special parking arrangements
were made with the police, the
market has its own parking space
on Jessie street for the use of patrons.

Tomorrow will be dedicated to the
women of the city. At exercises in
the morning Supervisor Margaret
Mary Morgan will preside. Speakers
on the program will be Mrs. W. B.
Hamilton, prominent clubwoman,
and Mrs. Bella de Graff.

**Watches, Diamonds, $1.00 a
Week. Your Credit Is Good**
Wear while paying. No red tape.
R. T. Brilliant, 780 Market, 2d floor.
—Advertisement.

At last tonsorial genius is appre-
ciated in a substantial way.

Jesse Whitehead, Palo Alto mil-
lionaire orchardist, has had no one
but Frank Schleigh of the Hotel St.
Francis shop cut his hair and shave
him for several years. But the trips
back and forth took too much of
Whitehead's valuable time.

Today Frank has Whitehead's
check with which to open a shop of
his own in Palo Alto, so that Whitehead will have his tonsorial expert
at hand at all times.

HOUSEWIVES TO GIVE 1922 REVUE

"Housewives' Follies of 1922," pre-
sented by an "all star cast," will be
the feature of the Christmas Jinx
of the Housewives' League tomorrow
afternoon at 2 o'clock, at the California Club, 1750 Clay street.

Mrs. Andrew Neuenburg is president of the league, and Mrs. H. A.
Byrnes is chairman of the day, which
will be given for members and their
friends.

A Food Emporium, which will of-
fer all sorts of food novelties for the
holiday season, will be one of the
features of the day.

Some of those in the all star cast
will be Mrs. Ida Finney Macville,
Mrs. Robert Dean, Mrs. J. C. Williams, Mrs. W. B. Hamilton, Mrs. A.
Pinther, Mrs. F. Wesley Carpenter,
Mrs. R. L. Lomax, Mrs. H. A. Byrnes
and Mrs. Hamilton Riggins.

Mrs. Katharine Musante will give
a series of dances. Miss F. V. Morker
will have charge of the cake table.
Mrs. Neuenburg, Mrs. Marie Wright,
Mrs. W. L. Bish of pies, and Mrs.
Byrnes and Mrs. E. F. Ingals of
other delicacies made by league
members.

Golden Gate Ferry Not Building in L. A.

Supervisor Eugene E. Schmitz is
on record today with an apology to
executives of the Golden Gate Ferry Company for questioning them
regarding rumors that a new boat
to be put into service by the company was being built at Los Angeles.

To explain the exact facts Harry
E. Speas, president of the ferry company, appeared before the board yesterday, advising it that the boat was
being built on San Francisco Bay,
despite the fact that it could be built
cheaper in Los Angeles and that ma-
chinery which could be purchased
cheaper in the East was being purchased in this city.

BELL CASE HALTE BY ILLNESS OF WILLIAMS

Owing to the sudden illness of
torney John T. Williams, of cou[n]
for the executors in the Teresa [Bell]
will contest, who was removed
St. Francis Hospital last night, [Su-]
perior Judge Frank H. Dunne [has]
put over the trial of the case u[ntil]
next Monday morning at 11 o'clo[ck.]

Counsel for the five Bell childr[en]
who are trying to break the will [is]
expected to complete their case [this]
morning.

The will giving the $850,000 [es-]
tate to charity declares the five ch[il-]
dren bearing the Bell name to be [dis-]
her issue. The contestants are [try-]
ing to prove Mrs. Bell was [of]
unsound when she wrote the will.

Counsel for the executors are [ex-]
pected to recall to the witness sta[nd]
Mrs. Susannah Jane Parks [and]
Mrs. Mary E. Salmond, who have [tes-]
tified that they were present at [the]
Octavia street "House of Myst[ery"]
when some of the Bell children [were]
born.

The first witness for the execu[tors]
will be T. Z. Blakeman who acted [as]
legal advisor for Mrs. Bell dur[ing]
her life. Blakeman is also associa[ted]
with the counsel for the executo[rs.]

SENATOR RIGDON DIES IN HOSPIT[AL]

State Senator E. S. Rigdon [of]
Cambria, San Luis Obispo cou[nty,]
died at the Stanford Hospital [last]
night after a brief illness from m[en-]
ingitis. Dr. R. L. Rigdon, local [phy-]
sician, his brother, was with [him]
when he passed away. Mrs. Rig[don]
and their son did not reach [him]
until later.

Rigdon, who was born in [?]
four years ago, was ser[ving]
his second term in the state sen[ate,]
having come up from the asse[mbly]
to which he was first elected [in]
1914. He was a rancher and b[usi-]
ness man at Cambria.

The senator's district inclu[ded]
San Luis Obispo and Monterey co[un-]
ties.

DIES OF BURNS

Mrs. Mary Johnston, 1123 Key [ave-]
nue, died at the San Francisco H[os-]
pital today from burns she rece[ived]
on Thanksgiving Day when a [coal]
oil stove in her home blew up. [She]
was 52 years old.

The vision for the market that was advertised to the public was "quality, purity and plenty" with a focus on feeding the people of San Francisco unadulterated and healthy food. Pictured on the left is a newspaper clipping from the *San Francisco Call and Post* on December 14, 1922, discussing the grand opening of the Crystal Palace Market. The newspaper reported that the market was flooded by locals on the first day. The opening of the market was accompanied by a welcome speech by Mayor Rolph. It also talks about the special feature of the market: the call boys who were on hand to carry the bundles of purchasers to their cars and the street cars. It also says that the second day would be dedicated to women.

The opening of the Crystal Palace Market was planned as a two-day event. The second day of the opening was dedicated to the women of the city. This advertisement in the *San Francisco Call and Post* on December 14, 1922, was targeted at the housewives of San Francisco. The event was hosted a day after the grand opening by a female supervisor, and prominent women of the city were invited as speakers.

When the market first opened on Eighth and Market Streets, streetcars were a common feature. The Crystal Palace Market was the first market to have a designated parking spot for its patrons, as seen in this 1953 photograph taken from Eighth Street; it shows the rear entrance that is also part of the 55,000-square-foot parking lot. The Crystal Palace Market was owned by the Rousseau brothers until 1925 and was sold to Emporium-Capwell in 1926. In 1944, the Crystal Palace Market was bought by 33-year-old Joseph Long of Alameda of the business Long Appliances.

Pictured here is an article from the *San Francisco Chronicle* in October 1922 showing the artistic rendering of the Crystal Palace Market with two entrances, one on Market Street and one on Eighth Street. This building was unique for its time because it provided ample parking, both on Market Street and Mission Street at the back. The parking on Market Street was sold to other businesses over the years to construct more buildings along Market Street.

The Crystal Palace Market was famous for its iconic bold signage, as seen in this photograph showcasing advertisements of several popular shops inside the market.

One of the main features of the Crystal Palace Market was its sprawling parking lot with thousands of parking spots. This enabled shoppers from every corner of the city to access the market. Pictured here is the massive parking lot at the Crystal Palace Market with the dome of San Francisco City Hall and Hotel Whitmore seen in the background on September 29, 1954.

Seen here is the panoramic view of Market Street during a parade in the late 1920s. The ferry building can be seen in the back, with the iconic Crystal Palace Market sign in the front. Over the years, this location was witness to several prominent parades and community events.

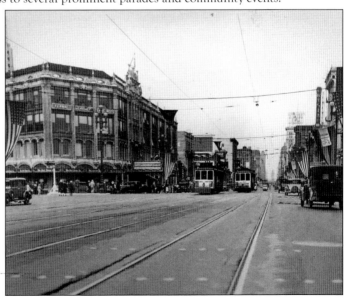

Pictured here is the view of the Crystal Palace Market and the historic Orpheum Theatre across Market Street. Orpheum Theatre opened four years after the Crystal Palace Market opened, thus making the intersection of Eighth and Market Street one of the most sought-after real estate locations in San Francisco in the 1920s.

This photograph shows the view of Market and Grove Streets, looking southeast at the outbound No. 21 streetcar on Eighth Street. The photograph shows the accessibility of the Crystal Palace Market and also gives a glimpse of the parking wall of the market, which was often used for advertisements.

Seen here is the 1927 photograph of Market and Eighth Streets with streetcar and car access. It shows a street with heavy foot and vehicular traffic. The iconic Crystal Palace Market sign can also be seen.

The location of Crystal Palace Market was surrounded by several prominent theaters and event venues. Some of the prominent buildings that opened in the year 1922 were the Paramount Theatre and the Warfield, as seen in this 1948 photograph. It also shows the first day when the brand-new white and green gasoline buses and trolleys started running on Market Street.

This 1953 image shows the parking wall with advertisements on the right and the historic Orpheum Theatre on the left, as well as the iconic location of the Crystal Palace Market.

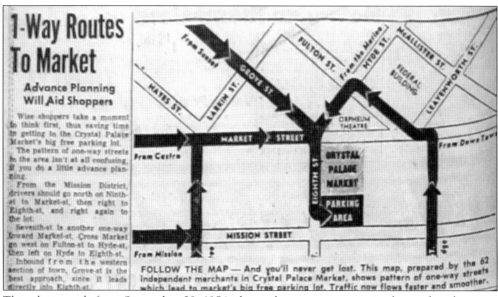

1-Way Routes To Market

Advance Planning Will Aid Shoppers

Wise shoppers take a moment to think first, thus saving time in getting to the Crystal Palace Market's big free parking lot.

The pattern of one-way streets in the area isn't at all confusing, if you do a little advance planning.

From the Mission District, drivers should go north on Ninth-st to Market-st, then right to Eighth-st, and right again to the lot.

Seventh-st is another one-way toward Market-st. Cross streets go west on Fulton-st to Hyde-st, then left on Hyde to Eighth-st.

Inbound from the western section of town, Grove-st is the best approach, since it leads directly into Eighth-st.

FOLLOW THE MAP — And you'll never get lost. This map, prepared by the 62 independent merchants in Crystal Palace Market, shows pattern of one-way streets which lead to market's big free parking lot. Traffic now flows faster and smoother.

This photograph from September 29, 1954, shows the one-way routes to the market that were highlighted and advertised in newspapers to assist patrons who wanted to visit and help them utilize the free parking that the market provided.

This photograph from Eighth Street taken on June 3, 1958, shows the rear entrance with the 55,000-square-foot Crystal Palace Market parking lot continuing in the rear. Over the years, more entry and exit points were added to the Crystal Palace Market for the ease of customers.

Three

PEOPLE AND
THE BUSINESSES

The Crystal Palace Market was a one-stop shop for exotic goods imported from all over the world. This image from February 26, 1953, shows a line of customers waiting for the market to open for New Zealand beef. The newspaper excerpt describes this scene as "WAITING—Here is a portion of the lineup of customers for New Zealand beef waiting for Roy's Meats in the Crystal Palace Market to open today. By 10 a.m. the line had grown to 550 people and extended down Market street to the Embassy Theater."

The Crystal Palace Market had six butcher shops. The range of meats that were offered to a customer was economically scaled cuts to highly priced quality meats. The Crystal Palace Market prided itself in being able to cater to both budget-conscious customers and customers who were willing to pay a premium for luxury high-quality meats. Pictured here is an ad for the meat market from the *Humboldt Times* on July 4, 1924, when the meat market first opened, highlighting the high quality and sanitary meats.

Pictured here are customers purchasing New Zealand beef from a meat counter at the Crystal Palace Market. A quote from the newspaper on February 26, 1953, reads, "GOING STRONG—Three hours after the sale of New Zealand beef started at the Crystal Palace Market today there was a sizable crowd clustered about the meat counter waiting for a chance to buy 39¢ a pound steak. Here's a part of the meat-hungry mob."

This photograph from February 26, 1953, shows Mrs. Earl Hascall holding her sixth-month-old baby Mary and a slab of New Zealand beef bought at the Crystal Palace Market. The news copy for this photograph reads, "AT LAST—Mrs. Earl Hascall, wife of an Air Force corporal, smiles at some of the New Zealand beef she bought at low cost today in the Crystal Palace Market. She's holding baby Mary, 6 months, just as she did for the two hours she waited in line."

Pictured here is the line of customers at the meat market in the Crystal Palace Market on June 3, 1946, which was known for the popular Roy's Meat stand and several meat stores that sold exotic meats and spices.

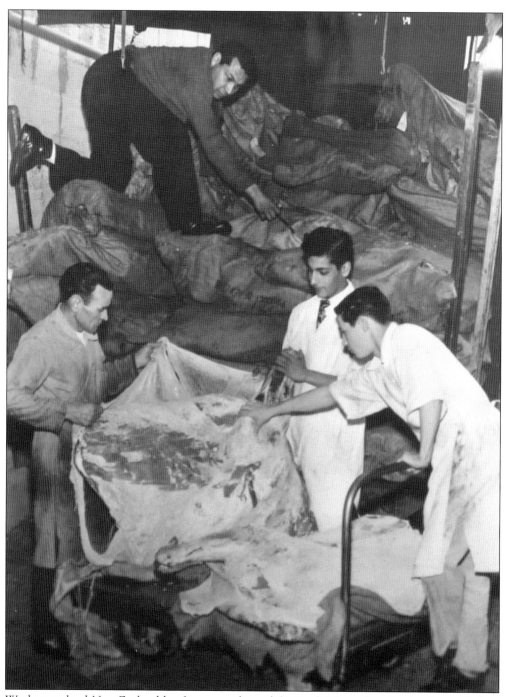

Workers unload New Zealand beef carcasses bound for Roy's Meats shop in the Crystal Palace Market. The news copy for this photograph reads, "NEW ZEALAND BEEF—Workers in Roy's Meats unload New Zealand beef carcasses preparatory to putting the meat on sale today at the two Roy's Meats shops, in the Crystal Palace Markets and the Annex Market."

Andre La Forgia stands behind a meat counter at the Crystal Palace Market on April 27, 1959. There were over 100 varieties of sausages offered at the market, which included a variety of imported sausages from fresh to dry sausages. The market sold a variety of sausages and the customers could try a range of local and imported sausages, from coppa veneziane, kishka, pinklewurst, salsicce, chorizos, to pepperoni.

Pictured here are Marston Fay and Sheldon Appleby on April 14, 1954, making sausages and waiting on customers at the Crystal Palace Market. The news copy for this photograph reads, "FINE SAUSAGE—Marston Fay and Sheldon Appleby, working in a glass-enclosed room, wait on customers, between rounds of turning out huge batches of bulk and link port sausages in Crystal Palace Market. Mouth watering?"

Pictured here is the Marion Silva meat department at the Crystal Palace Market, which sold exotic varieties of meat like the Alaskan reindeer meat seen in this photograph. The Marion Silva meat counter was one of the prominent meat counters of the market with extravagant displays of imported and exotic meats.

Crystal Market Palace was not only famous for its meat shops, but also featured three fish counters serving imported fish and seafood, like smoked oysters and crab meat from Japan, deep blue lobsters from South Africa, and halibut from Alaska. Pictured here is the fish counter at the Crystal Palace Market in April 1955.

The market was famous for selling imported ham and cold cuts at affordable prices with multiple meat counters daily serving hundreds of customers. There were several seasonal and specialty food items that were sold for limited periods at the market and specialty meats were one of those items. This photograph from September 30, 1953, shows a woman selling hams and packaged meats at the Crystal Palace Market, showcasing the variety of meats sold at the market, which included smoked sausages, seen on the right; canned ham in the background; and fresh and packaged ham in the front.

The slogan of the Crystal Palace Market was "Good meat for everyone—and at prices each can afford to pay." The shops in the meat market were arranged so that the meat buyer could choose their own quality and price from the fine, economically scaled cuts to the highest quality meats. The poultry department of the market prided itself in selling the most sanitary meat and preserving meat in state-of-the-art storages so that the customer could buy the best and healthiest quality meats. This photograph from November 17, 1954, shows the poultry department at the Crystal Palace Market manned by Tony Zanca's son.

There were several counters in the poultry section that catered to the tastes of customers that were specifically looking for premium cuts of meat during the holiday season. Emmett Rose's meat counter was one of the counters that served premium beef cuts for such customers. Pictured here is Emmett Rose standing behind a meat counter at the Crystal Palace Market, selling premium beef on November 17, 1954, during the Thanksgiving sale week.

The Crystal Palace Market had six butcher counters for customers to choose from. Pictured here on September 30, 1953, is one of the six meat counters, and also one of the most popular counters, called Roy's Meats at the Crystal Palace Market, serving exotic cuts of meats.

More than 215,000 eggs were sold each week at the Crystal Palace Market. Every egg was inspected for freshness, and the eggs ran through a cleaning machine. The complete assortment of eggs in the egg department included small, mediums, large, extra-large, jumbos, double yolks, ducks, turkeys, and brown and whites. In this photograph from September 30, 1953, is an employee working behind a counter in the dairy department at the Crystal Palace Market. To make sure that the customers always received quality eggs, they were only brought from local businesses in Santa Rosa and Petaluma daily by the department's truck service.

A staff of 10 employees maintained the egg department, and the egg section was licensed by the State of California and the City of San Francisco to conform to the strict regulations and health inspections on an average of twice a week. On arrival, eggs were placed on conveyor belts. The belts passed the scales, which weighed the eggs and sent them through the graded channels to the candling machines, where they were channeled through the ultraviolet candling light to detect sour eggs. After this, experienced counter girls placed them on shelves and into cartons of respective grades and quality. The eggs were then finally stacked on the counters for sale. Pictured here is a woman operating an egg-packaging machine at the Crystal Palace Market on September 29, 1954.

Imports from 37 countries were sold at the Crystal Palace Market. The nations represented in the market ranged from Algeria to Switzerland. Pictured here is the interior of the Crystal Palace Market in September 1953, with dried fruit and nuts counters on the left, bakeries in the background, and specialty goods on the right and front.

The photograph from the 1940s shows advertisements on the parking wall of the Crystal Palace Market. This prize-winning photograph was taken by John Gutmann. It was part of the photography exhibition Image of Freedom held from October 29, 1941, to January 4, 1942, at the Museum of Modern Art, New York.

Dry fruits and nuts were one of the most-loved sections during holidays at the market. Families looking for high-quality dry fruits and nuts flocked to the market, where these were sold at affordable prices. Pictured here is the dried fruits department at the Crystal Palace Market on November 17, 1954.

The Crystal Palace Market had an extensive fruit department with fruits imported from all over the world available at affordable prices for customers. The market featured imported fruits like bananas from Mexico and pineapples from Hawaii. Pictured here on April 6, 1955, showing the fruit on display at the market. The news copy for this photograph reads, "FROM ABOARD—If you think you know all of these fruits, you may be mistaken. Many are rare imports."

Pictured here is one of the food vendors named Pete Giannini arranging avocados at the market. The news copy for this photograph reads, "NEW SHIPMENTS—It's avocado time, and thousands of them are being brought in for display in the market."

This photograph shows the bulk food section of the market in September 1953. The market boasted affordable prices for all goods, and the bulk section catered to people with big families or tighter budgets.

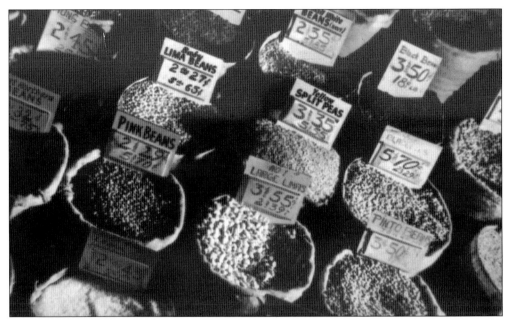

Pictured here are bulk foods on display at the Crystal Palace Market in September 1954. The Crystal Palace Market encouraged customers to save money by buying dried food supplies in bulk. The news copy for this photograph reads, "BULK PRODUCTS—This shows just some of many products available in bulk form at the Crystal Palace."

The Honey Concession stand was one of the most popular stands at the market. The variety of honey was displayed in larger glass vats with appropriate lighting effects. The variety of honey offered at the market ranged from clover, wildflowers, sage, and alfalfa. Pictured here is honey on sale at the Crystal Palace Market on September 30, 1953.

Pictured here is the produce department at the Crystal Palace Market. There were several produce counters in the market which sold products from other countries. Roquefort cheese, liver pate, mushrooms (cultivated and wild), sardines, cocktail onions, Hennessy cognac, Benedictine, and Marcel Pierre champagne were imported from France. From England, kippered herring, bouillon cubes, two brands of gin, berry preserves, and marmalade were imported.

There were several exotic cheeses that were sold at the market. Esrom, Kuminost, Taffelost, Tilset, Samsoe, blue, pilsen, and Port Salut cheese from Denmark; feta from Greece; Rikost and Primost from Sweden; Bel Paese, Provolone and Gorgonzola from Italy; Gjetost, Nokkelost, Gammelost, and goat cheese from Norway; Gruyere, Emmentaler, and Swiss cheese from Switzerland; Limburger cheese from Germany; Edam cheese, Eru mild cheese, and gouda from Holland were some of the imported cheeses that were sold at the market. Pictured here is the cheese counter at the Crystal Palace Market on November 17, 1954.

Pictured here is a photograph of the cheese department at the Crystal Palace Market from April 6, 1955. There were over 100 different varieties of cheeses featured in the market. There were several varieties of domestic and imported cheeses that were offered. One of the most expensive cheeses: the Gjetost which is a brown Norwegian cheese made of goat's milk or a blend of goat and cow's milk was sold in the Market for $1.50 per pound. The news copy describes this photograph as, "THE LONG, SHORT AND TALL—Name your cheese and the odds are 100 to 1 the Crystal Palace has it."

There were several local cheeses and cheeses from other states that were available at the Crystal Palace Market. Pictured here is the cheese department selling Wisconsin cheese at the market. The newspapers like the *San Francisco Chronicle* reported that Queen Mother Nazli of Egypt used to come to the Crystal Palace Market every day to shop when she made her home at the Fairmont Hotel.

Pictured here is Rawson Rack in the Crystal Palace Market's Standard Groceteria in November 1953. Rawson Rack was considered a modern shopping experience that was distributed to food stores only. Their main aim was to allow the shoppers to pick up their sundries and toiletries in the same place where they bought groceries instead of going to a pharmacy. The rack contained drug sundries, toiletries, cosmetics, shaving creams, and toothpaste. The news copy for this photograph reads, "FOR SHOPPING EASE—That's one of the main aims of this Rawson Rack in the Crystal Palace Market's Standard Groceteria. It enables the shopper to purchase any of hundreds of nationally advertised drugs or sundries while buying his groceries."

This photograph from September 30, 1953, shows the liquor department at the Crystal Palace Market selling a variety of wines, beers, and other liquors from local businesses as well as abroad. There were several seasonal liquors like bock beers that were available at the market over the years. One of the most popular beer stands at the market was the Anchor Steam Beer stand introduced in the market in 1953. Newspapers like the *San Francisco Chronicle* claimed that stream beer was one of San Francisco's oldest institutions, and it was kept alive at the Crystal Palace Market by the Anchor Brewing Company.

The Crystal Palace Market also featured specialty shops selling drugs for weight loss that were marketed toward women. Pictured here is a woman standing behind a counter at the Crystal Palace Market selling "dropex" weight-loss cocktail drops.

The Crystal Palace Market prided itself in having 12 eating places with a variety of specialties. The image shows the popular Frosty Ice Cream stand at the Crystal Palace Market on December 16, 1952. The decorations were a part of the Christmas market. The news copy for this photograph says, "DECORATED—The Crystal Palace Market is putting on its customary Christmas show. Typical decorations are these festooning the Frosty Ice Cream stand in the market."

Pictured here is one of the bakeries inside the Crystal Palace Market on September 30, 1953. The market claimed that a customer could eat at a different restaurant, fountain, or lunch counter each day for 12 days without ever leaving the market. The market's Mexican restaurant featured a Mexican specialty every day, and the food was served by waitresses in native Mexican costumes. The Oasis fountain and lunch restaurant offered sandwiches, ice cream, and soft drinks until 2:00 p.m.

There was also a popular cafeteria called the Manning's Cafeteria that had existed in the market since the opening. Mannings offered breakfast and lunch and a variety of foods. Near Mannings was the Snack Bar for wrapped sandwiches, coffee, doughnuts, and other snacks.

Another variety of restaurant that the market had was the Salad Bowl, which served salads, healthy juices, fruit salads, and puddings made of prunes, applesauce, and healthy foods. Pictured here is Tropical Juice and Fruit Salad Bar at the Crystal Palace Market on December 16, 1953. The news copy for this photograph reads, "QUICK SNACK—Shoppers rounding up goodies for that big Christmas dinner take time out for a bolstering sip of tropical juices or a tempting fruit salad." There was another restaurant called the Palace Gardens Restaurant and Bar, which was the only full-fledged bar in the market and served full meals with cocktails. One of the crowd favorites at this restaurant was "quick pup," a hot dog on a stick dipped in a special mix. The market also had an Italian restaurant called Joe's Spaghetti, which served spaghetti and several Italian dishes.

Pictured here are customers at the doughnut and coffee stand at the market. The news copy for this photograph read, "'COFFEE AND'—Here is one of the few, if not the only place, in San Francisco where coffee is still a nickel. It's in the Crystal Palace Market, of course, where else? One of the most popular spots in the market, the stand also offers 'Coffee and'—a cup of coffee and a doughnut—for only one thin dime." At the Doughnut bar, one of the food counters at the market, doughnuts were made fresh and were served with 5¢ coffee. The coffee shops were also accompanied by magazine shops at the market, which sold copies of the *New Yorker*.

One of the prominent types of businesses that operated in the Crystal Palace Market was catering for office and dinner parties. Pictured here are two employees standing behind the counter of the Family Corner delicatessen and catering counter at the Crystal Palace Market.

In 1955, due to public demand, the Crystal Palace Market management installed a new concession stand—a pizzeria—in the market. It was called Antonio's Casa di Pizza and was next to the Crystal Caterer's delicatessen department. It served authentic Italian pizza recipes prepared and baked on the premises. There were also single slices of pizza that were available ranging from 15¢ to 25¢. Pictured here is a photograph from September 28, 1955, of Frances Ketchum taking a pizza out of an oven at a pizza stand in the Crystal Palace Market.

Another restaurant called the Jumbo Lunch, which had existed since the opening of the market, sold a variety of wrapped sandwiches, root beer, milkshakes, and hamburgers. At the Dixie Lunch & Fountain, ice-cream products were one of the most popular items, apart from hamburgers, pies, and hot roast beef sandwiches. Pictured here is the ice-cream counter at the Crystal Palace Market in the 1950s.

The Crystal Palace Market had an extensive appliances store offering nationally known brand name products. The market had a complete range of appliances ranging from refrigerators, stoves, washers, dryers, ironers, and radio and television sets from America's leading manufacturers of the 1950s. This photograph from the 1950s shows an unidentified woman holding a toaster in the kitchen appliance department at the Crystal Palace Market.

This photograph from September 30, 1953, shows Long's Appliances displaying a range of gas stoves, refrigerators, and radios in the back of the Crystal Palace Market. The market also had a sports shop catering to hobbies like fishing, hunting, baseball, and bowling to name a few. The Crystal Palace housewares section and sporting goods can also be seen in the background.

This photograph from April 14, 1954, shows the fishing supply department at the Crystal Palace Market. The fishing supply store featured a wide range of equipment for an angler from featherweight trout rods to heavy tackle rods for deep-water fishing. Apart from stores selling a variety of products, the market also had several utility shops, like the shoe repair shop offering customers speedy, efficient service in half-soling, reheeling, and other related needs.

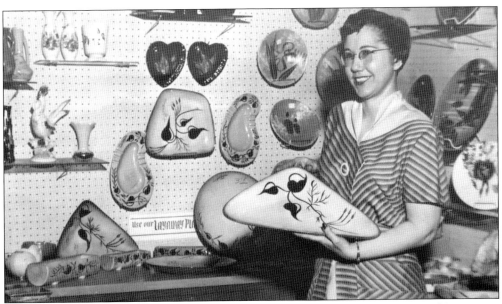

The Crystal Palace Market featured 65 variety shops ranging from home décor and houseware stores to beauty parlors, pet stores, and locksmith services. Pictured here is a woman holding a large ashtray at the Crystal Palace Market. There was also a nursery at the Crystal Palace Market where customers could buy flowers and plants for gifting.

PAYROLL CHECKS CASHED   PAYROLL CHECKS

BUY MONEY ORDERS HERE

WE REQUIRE
NAME & ADDRESS
INDORSEMENTS
* ON ALL CHECKS
BEFORE CASHING

Buy
BANK OF AMERICA
TRAVELERS CHEQUES
here!

OXCO Floor Sweeps

Charges
10¢

The Crystal Palace Market also provided a special payroll check cashing booth for the convenience of the customers in the market which went into operation in July 1953. It was inaugurated when the banks eliminated Saturday business hours. An employee was on duty throughout the day at this booth to cash checks, and a fee of 10¢ per check was charged to help pay for the special service. Money orders were also sold at the booth for the convenience of the customers. The market spokesperson told the news reporters that the booth was set up specifically as a "convenience to our customers, not to make money." The news copy for this photograph reads, "NOT CLOSED SATURDAYS—For the convenience of customers, the Crystal Palace Market provides this special payroll check cashing booth. It's open six days a week, from 9:30 a.m. to 5:45 p.m. and charges 10¢ a check for the service."

Four

EVENTS AND CELEBRATIONS

Crystal Palace Market was famous for holding extravagant sales and events for the public especially in the 1950s to maintain the connection of the community to the market. Pictured here is a crowd of customers in the wine section of the market during the 31st birthday anniversary sale in 1953, with prices slashed up to 30–40 percent. For the 31st birthday anniversary sale, the theme was Hawaiian. There were Hawaiian huts displaying colorful displays of pineapples, papaya, and avocado with cooking demonstrations. In every anniversary sale, new products were introduced in the market. In the 31st birthday-anniversary event, steam beer was introduced to the customers.

One of the big features of the Crystal Palace Market's 32nd-anniversary sale was entertainment programs featuring Food Quiz and Big Jim DeNoon, "the Giant of Western Swing." The event was sponsored by the William Perry Food Brokerage Co., a food-product business. Customers were selected from the market to be interviewed by quizmaster Dave Stone, with prizes of merchandise going to the winners. Pictured here is Big Jim DeNoon playing guitar for customers at the Crystal Palace Market on October 3, 1955, as part of the Crystal Palace Market's 32nd-anniversary sale. The news articles reported that the 32nd-anniversary sale witnessed thousands of customers flocking to the businesses at the market.

Apart from the annual Crystal Palace Market anniversary sales, events like Thanksgiving and Christmas were the most popular events at the market. Several prominent newspapers like the *San Francisco News* carried advertisements weeks in advance for fancy turkeys, hickory-smoked pork sausage, and beef roast that were sold at the market. Pictured here are three butchers standing behind the counter of the poultry department at the Crystal Palace Market on September 30, 1953.

Pictured here are customers choosing a turkey from one of four poultry shops in the Crystal Palace Market. During events like Thanksgiving, anniversary, and Christmas sales, there were special shuttle buses that ran to the Eighth and Market Streets from Grove and Franklin Street passing through Market Street until Second Street. During these events, the market incentivized the customers to shop by providing them with free one-hour parking. Maps to access the Crystal Palace Market were advertised extensively during these events. The market also had 22 entrances that were provided for the convenience of the customers located on five different streets: Market, Mission, Eighth, Stevenson, and Jessie.

Christmas at the Crystal Palace Market was one of the most celebrated events in the market. From 1925 to the 1930s, a Christmas tree lot and auto were created on the south side of Market between Seventh and Eighth Streets to help with the customers. Seen in this photograph is the 35-foot-tall Christmas tree in the Crystal Palace Market in 1953.

The Crystal Palace Market was a one-stop shop for all Christmas shopping, including home decor, gift wrapping, and Christmas gifts with different price points that a customer could shop for. Pictured here is Marian Abrahamson holding a Christmas wreath at a flower stand in the Crystal Palace Market in 1953.

Pictured here is a woman shopping at the Herod's Variety Store at the Crystal Palace Market on December 16, 1953. The news copy for this image had a headline, "HOLIDAY DECORATIONS— Brightly colored Christmas tree lights, delicately tinted ornaments of all shapes and sizes and gay Christmas cards can be seen in tempting array in this glimpse of the bulging counters of Herod's Variety Store centrally located in Crystal Palace Market."

Pictured here is the display arranged by the Crystal Caterers' counter, one of the most popular caterers of the market in 1951. The whole market was decorated with holiday trimmings every Christmas and featured special holiday offerings by the different businesses in the market.

Pictured here are Frances Ketchum and Johanne Behrens standing behind the festively decorated Crystal Caterers counter at the Crystal Palace Market on December 16, 1953. Crystal Caterers was a popular business that supplied all the fixings for an office party, dinner, or picnic.

Christmas decorations in the market were also extended to the produce section. Seen here are the interiors of the Crystal Palace Market in 1953, showing the cross-section of the variety of holiday foods offered at the market. The popular bakery and the nuts section, fish, poultry, and the economic meat stands of the Crystal Palace Market are seen in the background.

Pictured here is the produce department of the Crystal Palace Market on December 16, 1953, with a "season's greetings" poster lining the produce aisle.

Pictured here is Gerbino's homemade cookies and candy counter at the Crystal Palace Market, which was a popular counter for children and parents. The picture shows special cookie and candy gift boxes for Christmas gifting.

In 1951, the Crystal Palace Market dressed up in holiday glitter and hosted two big annual Christmas parties for children from 10:00 to 11:00 a.m. and 2:00 to 3:00 p.m. on December 19. Christmas parties at the Market were popular with the patrons and especially the kids. Pictured here is the "Santa Claus Party" at the Crystal Palace Market on December 18, 1951. The news copy for this image reads, "SANTA'S EVERYWHERE—Every time you turn around these days there's a new Santa Claus popping up. This one showed up today to delight youngsters at the Crystal Palace Market." The Santa Claus parties at the market had extensive Christmas decorations, gifts, novelties and candies for children, balloons, and music.

Thousands of customers and their kids flocked to the Santa Claus Party in the days leading to Christmas for photographs. Pictured here is a photograph from the Santa Claus Party at the Crystal Palace Market on December 23, 1952.

Crystal Palace Market was famous for its extravagant decorations for Christmas. Pictured here are the Christmas decorations on the roof of the Crystal Palace Market on December 7, 1950. The news copy for this photograph reads, "Santa Claus, a traditional fixture atop the roof of the Crystal Palace Market every year at this time, has increased his sleigh's horse—er deerpower by two this season. Now they're all there—Dasher, Prancer, Donder and Blitzen, Cupid, Comet, Dancer and Vixen." ("Donder" was the original name for Donner in Clement Clarke Moore's "A Visit from St. Nicholas.")

Five

END OF AN ERA

By the 1950s, with more people moving to the suburbs, the footfall of Crystal Palace Market and several buildings in the downtown were drastically reduced. Eventually, in 1959, the owner J.M. Long decided to sell the 4.5-acre Crystal Palace Market site to Del Webb who was a building magnate of the 1950s and one of the owners of the New York Yankees baseball team. This 1959 photograph was taken when several businesses were declaring final sales. The news copy for this image in the *San Francisco Call* reads, "The fancied echo of uncounted millions of shuffling feet will be all that remains in the Crystal Palace Market when the doors close tonight and it assumes a ghost-like appearance while awaiting arrival of the wreckers."

Pictured here is the last day of the Crystal Palace Market on August 3, 1959. The image shows a row of empty shelves with almost all of the goods sold by the final day. The words accompanied by this picture in the news copy state, "THERE WEREN'T MANY BARGAINS LEFT—Closing time saw the shelves nearly empty."

Pictured here are the moments of the last day of the Crystal Palace Market. There were several business owners who had shops in the market for 36 years, and this photograph shows the camaraderie and friendships that were built in the market. Seen in this image are Tony Zanca on the far right and a group making a toast on the last day of business at the Crystal Palace Market. The news copy headline for this image reads, "TONY ZANCA (FAR RIGHT) CLOSES HIS POULTRY STAND—After 36 years, a toast at a lively wake."

Pictured here is the rush of people flocking to the meat businesses on their last day of business. The meat stands were one of the most popular businesses of the Crystal Palace Market, which is evident in this image. The news copy of the headline for this photograph reads "A LAST-MINUTE SALE AT A MEAT STAND— Trade was brisk as customers flowed in for final shopping."

Pictured here is the cash register on sale on the final day of business at the market. The market employed 300 people and had more than 75 businesses. Everything was on sale on the final day of the market, including store equipment.

This image shows the empty interiors of the Crystal Palace Market before it was demolished. The newspapers reported that on the final day, everything was sold-out as the market closed its doors after 36 years. The news copy headlines for this image read, "GHOST-LIKE–Crystal Palace Market, which closed its doors to make way for an $8 million 400-room motor hotel, echoed to the tread of wreckers today as it took on the appearance of a vacant barn. Long gone is the bustle of hurrying feet, the calls of merchants hawking their wares and the scores of businesses which featured delicacies from the four corners of the globe."

Pictured here is the day when the wrecker's steel ball demolished the Crystal Palace Market in September 1959. The *San Francisco Call* reported that the wreckers took over the market with a 2,800-pound battering ram, exactly one month after it closed its doors after serving two generations of San Francisco and the Bay Area residents. The massive structure paved the way for the next building on the corner of Eighth and Market Streets.

The new building proposed on the market site was an $8 million motor hotel/motel with luxurious rooms, a swimming pool, and two garden courts. Pictured here is the construction of the new motel on the Crystal Palace Market site on September 17, 1960. San Franciscoo City Hall can be seen in the background. The motel was later converted into residences and was called Del Webb's Townehouse.

Pictured here is the photograph looking northward at the completed Del Webb's Townehouse on May 9, 1961. The Bay Bridge can be seen in the distance. The building offered guests 400 luxurious, fully air-conditioned rooms, a beautiful Carriage Room restaurant and lounge, a coffeehouse, a garden terrace for lounging and dining, a heated swimming pool, and free parking for their cars on the hotel property. The motel was later converted into apartments and was bought by Angelo Sangiacomo, who owned Trinity Properties. The Trinity Place Apartments were developed on the site at Eighth and Market Streets in 2003 and took 19 years in the making. In March 2022, a Whole Foods Market stands on the corner of Eighth and Market.

DISCOVER THOUSANDS OF LOCAL HISTORY BOOKS
FEATURING MILLIONS OF VINTAGE IMAGES

Arcadia Publishing, the leading local history publisher in the United States, is committed to making history accessible and meaningful through publishing books that celebrate and preserve the heritage of America's people and places.

Find more books like this at
www.arcadiapublishing.com

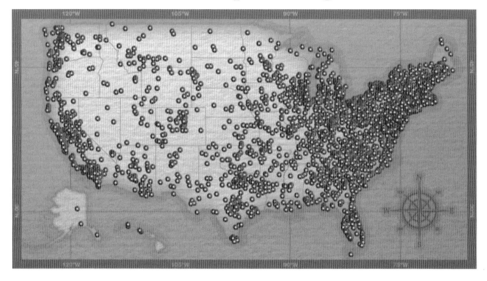

Search for your hometown history, your old stomping grounds, and even your favorite sports team.

Consistent with our mission to preserve history on a local level, this book was printed in South Carolina on American-made paper and manufactured entirely in the United States. Products carrying the accredited Forest Stewardship Council (FSC) label are printed on 100 percent FSC-certified paper.

MADE IN THE USA